The Black Man in America
1905–1932

The Black Man in America
1905–1932

by Florence Jackson

illustrated with photographs and contemporary drawings

Franklin Watts, Inc.
New York | 1974

Frontispiece – A painting by Jacob Lawrence
depicting the antagonism between white and black
workers that erupted into race riots in major cities
throughout the country during 1919.

Library of Congress Cataloging in Publication Data

Jackson, Florence.
    The Black man in America, 1905-1932.

    SUMMARY: Traces the history of blacks in the
United States from the Niagara Movement begun by
W. E. B. Du Bois, to Roosevelt's New Deal.
    1. Negroes–History—1877-1964—Juvenile
literature. [1. Negroes–History—1877-1964]
I. Title.
E185.6.J127 1974   917.3′06′96073   73-13931
ISBN 0-531-02667-1

Contents

The Black Man in America
1905–1932

From Movement to Organization

AT THE TURN OF THE TWENTIETH CENTURY, black people still were the victims of violence and during the first few years of the new century, the number of violent incidents increased. In desperation, a few black leaders felt they had to plan a program that would protect the masses of their people.

In 1905, the outstanding spokesman and thinker William E. B. Du Bois called for a meeting near Niagara Falls, Canada. Its purpose was to find ways of dealing with the many ills, including violence, that befell black people. Du Bois stated, "The time seems more than ripe for organized, determined and aggressive action on the part of men who believe in Negro freedom and growth . . ."

It was in this way that the Niagara Movement was established. In 1906, the second annual meeting of the movement was held at Harper's Ferry, Virginia. This location was chosen in memory of abolitionist John Brown, who had led an unsuccessful raid on the armory in an attempt to get arms for slaves. At the meeting, plans were made to continue the work of the Niagara Movement.

In 1907, Mary White Ovington, a white social worker, received an assignment from the *New York Evening Post* to cover the third annual meeting of the Niagara Movement. Mary Ovington was deeply moved by what she saw and heard.

Earlier experiences had made Mary Ovington aware of the poor treatment of black people. In the spring of 1906, W. E. B. Du Bois had invited her to visit him in Atlanta, Georgia. There, Mary Ovington saw segregation by law and general disrespect for black people.

William E. Burghardt Du Bois, the radical thinker whose call for a meeting near Niagara Falls, Canada, led to the establishment of the NAACP.

She also gained some understanding of the problems and tensions that were common in Southern cities.

The following winter, Mary Ovington returned to the South to gather more information about the life and treatment of black people for a survey she was making. When she returned home, Mary Ovington moved into the black community of San Juan Hill. She wanted to get a first-hand view of how black people lived in New York City. Mary Ovington found violence against blacks, lack of police protection, and no desire among city officials to end vice and crime in the black community. She also saw that working mothers had no one to care for their children during the day. And young people, generally, had no desire to develop careers because they would not be hired after finishing their training. In most cases, Mary Ovington found that the black man in the North was not allowed to develop his talents, compete for jobs, receive equal treatment, and care for his family like a white man. He was only allowed to be "half" a man. It was obvious that conditions in New York City were not much better than those in the South.

In August, 1908, William English Walling, a Southern journalist, described the horrors of two days of rioting in Springfield, Illinois. Two black men were lynched, four whites were killed, and more than seventy people were injured. Over one hundred people were arrested, but those who were thought to be the leaders of the white mob were never punished.

Mary Ovington read the account and decided that something had to be done. She wrote to Mr. Walling and suggested that they look for a way to help improve relations between black and white people in both the North and the South. Walling agreed. During the first week of January, 1909, Mary Ovington, William Walling, and Henry

Mary Ovington, a white social worker who, through an assignment, became deeply involved with black people, their struggle for better living conditions, and the establishment of the NAACP.

Moskovitz, a social worker for the New York City government, met at Walling's home to discuss the situation. They decided to urge prominent Americans to sign a document calling for a conference on the race problem.

The document, written by Oswald Garrison Villard, who was the publisher of the *New York Evening Post* as well as William Lloyd Garrison's grandson, was published in the *Evening Post* on February 12, 1909 — the 100th Anniversary of Abraham Lincoln's birth. A number of very well-known Americans signed the document. Among them were Jane Addams, social reformer and founder of Hull House; John Dewey, educator at Columbia University; William Lloyd Garrison, abolitionist and publisher; Francis J. Grimké, a leading black minister in Washington, D.C.; William Dean Howells, writer on social problems; J. G. Phelps Stokes, philanthropist; Lincoln Steffens, journalist; Ida B. Wells Barnett, journalist; Mary Church Terrell, a fighter for equal rights for women and black people; Bishop Alexander Walter, A. M. E. Zion Church; Rabbi Stephen S. Wise, reformer and Zionist leader; Mary E. Woolley, President of Mount Holyoke College; and William E. B. Du Bois.

During the conference, from May 30 to June 1, 1910, the Negro National Committee was formed. The following year, at the second annual meeting, the committee changed its name to the National Association for the Advancement of Colored People (NAACP). Although the organization was not incorporated until 1911, February 12, 1909 — the date that Oswald Garrison Villard's call for a conference was published — has always been considered founding date of the NAACP.

Practically the entire membership of the Niagara Movement, including W. E. B. Du Bois, joined the NAACP. Two leading black journalists, Monroe Trotter and Ida B. Wells Barnett, still distrustful of white leaders, refused to join the new organization.

The goals of the NAACP were "to promote equality of rights and eradicate caste or race prejudice among the citizens of the United States; to advance the interest of colored citizens; to secure for them impartial suffrage; and to increase their opportunities for securing justice in the courts, education for their children, employment according to their ability, and complete equality before the law."

The NAACP opened offices in New York City and began to work actively toward improving conditions for black people. They issued press releases to publicize injustices, and their legal department defended those who were unjustly charged. On November 10, 1909, the organization published the first issue of *The Crisis*.

W. E. B. Du Bois, who had resigned from his position at Atlanta University to work full time with the NAACP, was the editor of *The Crisis*. He stated in the first issue that *The Crisis* would stand for "the highest ideals of American democracy and for reasonable but earnest and persistent attempts to gain these rights and realize these ideals." By the end of the first year, *The Crisis* had about 12,000 readers.

Serving as ample justification of the need for the NAACP was Mary Ovington's survey of the condition of black people, published in 1911 after seven years of research. She named the book, *Half a Man: The Status of the Negro in New York*. Mary Ovington explained the title in the introduction to the book:

Six years ago I met a young colored man, a college student recently returned from Germany where he had been engaged in graduate work. He was born, he told me, in one of the Gulf states, and I questioned him as to whether he intended going back to the South to teach. His answer was in the negative. "My father has attained success in his native state," he said, "but when I ceased to be a boy, he advised me to live in the North where my manhood would be respected. He himself cannot continually endure the position in

THE CRISIS

A RECORD OF THE DARKER RACES

Volume One   NOVEMBER, 1910   Number One

Edited by W. E. BURGHARDT DU BOIS, with the co-operation of Oswald Garrison Villard,
J. Max Barber, Charles Edward Russell, Kelly Miller, W. S. Braithwaite and M. D. Maclean.

CONTENTS

PUBLISHED MONTHLY BY THE

National Association for the Advancement of Colored People

AT TWENTY VESEY STREET   NEW YORK CITY

ONE DOLLAR A YEAR   TEN CENTS A COPY

which he is placed, and in the summer he comes North to be a man. "No," correcting himself, "to be half a man. A Negro is wholly a man only in Europe."

Half a man! During the six years that I have been in touch with the problem of the Negro in New York this characterization has grown in significance to me.

Jobs for Migrants

IN EFFORTS TO FULFILL ITS STATED GOALS, the NAACP encouraged businesses to hire black migrants; worked to end lynchings, segregation, and discrimination; and tried to obtain voting rights for black people. Working toward these aims left little time to develop an effective program to improve the economic conditions of black people.

There were, however, two organizations that were established to help the growing number of black people in Northern cities find jobs. They were the Committee for Improving Industrial Conditions of Negroes in New York and the National League for the Protection of Colored Women.

At about the same time, George Edmund Haynes, a young black graduate student at Columbia University, did a study of the social and economic conditions of black people in New York City in 1909–10. The results of the study were given to the two organizations. The findings were of such great interest that a committee was formed to develop a program to improve the conditions mentioned in Haynes's study.

As the program took form, a need for an organization developed.

The first issue of <u>The Crisis</u>, the magazine published by the NAACP and edited by W.E.B. Du Bois.

Therefore, in 1911, the committee and the two existing organizations joined together to become the National League on Urban Conditions among Negroes. And Haynes became one of the executive officers. Later, the organization was called the National Urban League.

The main purposes of the National Urban League were to find opportunities in industry for black people and to help those who were new to the city adjust to urban life. The League also provided opportunities for the training of social workers. Fellowships were given to young black men and women to help support them while they studied. A number of leading black social workers came out of this program.

Presidents Play Politics

DURING THE EARLY 1900's, BLACK PEOPLE had little reason to look to United States political leaders with hope or with trust. Theodore Roosevelt, for example, who became President in 1901, had praised the black soldiers of the Ninth and Tenth Cavalries who fought with his Rough Riders during the Spanish-American War; but in 1899, he wrote an article for *Scribner's* magazine in which he made unfavorable comments about the same black soldiers. This was only one of several acts in which Roosevelt accepted and then rejected black people.

About a month after becoming President, Roosevelt invited Booker T. Washington to the White House and had lunch with him during an interview. White Southerners were outraged at the thought of a black man dining at the White House. But white Southerners had nothing to fear. Within a few years, Roosevelt adopted a hands-off policy toward the South and did little to help blacks.

George Edmund Haynes, co-founder and chief-executive of the National Urban League.

The next President, William Howard Taft, also generally did nothing to help black people. Though Taft did appoint William H. Lewis, a black man, as assistant attorney general, he stopped appointing blacks to federal positions in the South. In fact, Taft felt that the only way to solve the race problem was to send blacks out of the country.

In 1912, both Roosevelt and Taft sought the nomination as the Republican candidate for the Presidency. When Roosevelt failed to get Republican support, he campaigned on a Progressive Party platform. Again, Roosevelt showed little regard for black people. When the NAACP submitted a statement to be included in the Progressive Party platform, Roosevelt allowed the Southern white delegates not only to refuse to accept the statement but also to bar some of the black delegates from the convention.

The Democratic nominee was Woodrow Wilson. He said:

I want to assure them [black people] that should I become President of the United States they may count upon me for absolute fair dealing, for everything by which I could assist in advancing the interests of their race in the United States.

Woodrow Wilson won the election. Black people watched and waited. Some people felt that Wilson really wanted to be fair to blacks, but that others in government did not. Congress aimed to keep the two races apart. The largest number of bills against black people in the United States history were proposed during President Wilson's administration. There were bills to segregate blacks on transportation facilities in Washington, D.C.; to keep black men from getting commissions in the Army and Navy; to segregate facilities for

William H. Lewis: after his appointment as assistant attorney general by President Taft in 1911, little effort was made by the government to aid black people.

black and white federal employees; and to bar immigrants who were black or descendants of blacks. Finally, President Wilson, himself, issued an executive order that resulted in segregated lunch and restroom facilities for most black federal employees.

Again, black people had been led to believe they would receive fair treatment from the President of the United States. Instead, they found that the president had helped to move them backward in their struggle for equal rights.

War Brings Changes

WORLD WAR I BEGAN IN EUROPE IN 1914. Most black people felt that there was little cause to worry about the war. They had to direct their attention to the whites who were keeping them from participating fully in American life. That in itself was a tough battle.

It seems as though it was not enough for a white person to be prejudiced against blacks. He had to convince others that his views were "right." One way to increase prejudice was to spread false information. The motion picture *Birth of a Nation*, for example, created bad feelings and prejudice against blacks. In 1915, it was shown in movie houses throughout the United States. The film was totally anti-black. It told an untrue story of how black people gained freedom and voting rights. It also appealed to the already negative attitudes of those whites who wished to think that white women should fear black men.

It is not certain that the film caused whites to become more violent against blacks. But anti-black violence did increase after its appearance. Sixty-nine lynchings occurred that year. The Ku Klux Klan became very active again. In addition, black leader Booker T. Washington, whose ideas appealed to many whites, died that November. The future for black Americans seemed bleak.

12

In the meantime, the war in Europe had spread. President Woodrow Wilson's efforts to keep America out of the war had failed. And on April 6, 1917, Congress declared war on Germany. As in previous wars, black men volunteered for service, and again, they were at first refused. However, the passage of the Selective Service Act in May, 1917 covered all Americans. Therefore black men were allowed to enlist. Over two million black men registered, and about 367,000 were called into service.

Black soldiers were trained in segregated camps in America. Some divisions were divided among several different training camps because no provisions were made to keep them together. Moreover, Southerners objected to black Northerners being trained in the South. However, the pressures of providing men for service made Army authorities disregard the objections and some black soldiers received training in the South.

About 50,000 black soldiers, more than one third of the American troops, fought in Europe. Some of them were placed in French divisions. They found that the French soldiers and civilians accepted them and treated them as equals. White American soldiers, however, did not like to see the black solders being readily accepted by the French. Some of the whites told the French people that the black soldiers could not be treated as equals and that in America whites had to lynch and burn blacks to keep them in their place. United States General James Erwin even issued an order that black soldiers were not to associate with French women. In addition, in August, 1918, a leaflet was circulated among the French titled "Secret Information Concerning Black Troops." It stated that if blacks and whites were not kept separated, blacks would assault white women. The French soldiers and civilians, however, did not take the warning seriously, and they continued to associate with the black soldiers.

Back home, on July 2, 1917, a bloody riot broke out in East St. Louis, Illinois, when black workers were hired to break a factory strike. At least thirty-nine blacks and eight whites were killed. In addition, hundreds of black people were injured and about six hundred were left homeless. Local labor leaders were blamed by some people for the riot. It was said that blacks who had recently arrived in the city accepted jobs at lower wages than whites. Some people said that the union leaders provoked anti-black hysteria.

A number of black people protested the riot. Later that month in New York City, black people marched to muffled drum beats in what has become known as the Silent Protest Parade. *The New York American* newspaper reported that fifteen thousand black people marched in the parade. One banner read, "Mr. President, why not make America safe for democracy?" Another said, "Bring Democracy to America Before You Carry It to Europe."

During this time, German propaganda was being circulated in the United States in an attempt to win over black people. Some of the propaganda directed toward blacks said that in Germany blacks and whites were equal and that if Germany won the war, the rights of black people around the world would be equal to those of the whites.

The disturbances in East St. Louis, the German propaganda, and the many injustices that both black civilians and soldiers lived through could have made black people turn against America. Instead, they supported the war for democracy. An example of a call for unity among blacks and whites was a stirring editorial written by W. E. B. Du Bois and published in the NAACP publication, *The Crisis,* July, 1918. Du Bois wrote:

> *. . . That which the German power represents today spells death to the aspirations of Negroes and all darker races for equality, freedom and democracy. Let us not hesitate. Let us, while this war*

At the beginning of World War I, black men — seen here fighting in a trench — were denied the right to serve in the armed forces.

14

East St. Louis, Ill., *May 23, 1917.*

To the Delegates to the Central Trades and Labor Union.

Greeting: The immigration of the southern Negro into our city for the past eight months has reached the point where drastic action must be taken if we intend to work and live peaceably in this community.

Since this influx of undesirable Negroes has started, no less than 10,000 have come into this locality.

These men are being used to the detriment of our white citizens by some of the capitalists and a few of the real estate owners.

On next Monday evening the entire body of delegates to the Central Trades and Labor Union will call upon the mayor and city council and demand that they take some action to retard this growing menace and also devise a way to get rid of a certion portion of those who are already here.

This is not a protest against the Negro who has been a long resident of East St. Louis and is a law-abiding citizen.

We earnestly request that you be in attendance on next Monday evening at 8 o'clock, at 137 Collinsville Avenue, where we will meet and then go to the city hall.

This is more important than any local meeting, so be sure you are there.

Fraternally,

Central Trades and Labor Union.

515

lasts, forget our special grievances and close our ranks shoulder to shoulder with our own white fellow citizens and the allied nations that are fighting for democracy. We make no ordinary sacrifice, but we make it gladly and willingly with our eyes lifted to the hills.

But just being enlisted men did not please black soldiers. They also wanted to train as officers. Up to that time, Congress had provided for the training of only white officers. To correct the situation, a committee from the NAACP went to Washington to speak to military authorities on behalf of black enlisted men. But they were unsuccessful.

Black college students realized the importance of having black officers. Soon they began to call for officers' training for black men. Finally, General Leonard Wood said that if 206 black college men could be found, he would see that they had a training camp. Within ten days, about 1,500 black college men signed up to receive officers' training.

Black people, however, did not want a separate officers' training camp. They said that such a camp only supported segregation. But Joel Spingarn, head of the NAACP committee that had asked General Wood to provide training for black officers, said that the black officers' training camp would help to fight segregation. He pointed out that each black candidate would have an equal chance at promotion. Furthermore, it would be fulfilling Southern wishes if black men did not receive this level of military training.

Training began and on October 15, 1917, black men received commissions. There were 106 captains, 329 first lieutenants, and 204

Above: a notice expressing the anti-black attitude of organized labor, which helped provoke violent riots in East St. Louis, 1917. Below: The Silent Protest Parade of black people in New York City protesting the East St. Louis riots. Posters point out the contributions of black people to America and the unfair treatment they received.

second lieutenants, making a total of 639 black officers. Although there were training camps for black officers, a few black men received commissions in white camps. Others prepared themselves on campuses through Students' Army Training Corps and Reserve Officers' Training Corps.

When the war ended in 1918, black men had served in every branch of the armed forces. They were, however, barred from becoming pilots. Some served in the Navy, but only in jobs that were considered to be the lowest types. None were allowed to serve in the Marines. But many received awards for distinguished service. Two outstanding black soldiers were Henry Johnson and Needham Roberts, who were the first Americans to receive France's highest honor for bravery, the *Croix de Guerre.*

The Great Northern Drive

As WORLD WAR I SPREAD THROUGHOUT EUROPE, immigration to the United States dwindled. Some Europeans who had earlier immigrated to the United States returned to their native lands to join the defense of their native countries.

At the same time, the United States was becoming a source of food and industrial products for the nations at war. American farmers planted more crops, and many industrial plants turned to the production of war equipment.

As the fighting in Europe progressed, the demand for war materials grew. As a result, production increased and new jobs were created. Since so many factory jobs had been filled by European immigrants, the decrease in their number, combined with the demand for more goods, left the factories with openings for new workers.

Northern industrialists looked to the South to fulfill their labor needs. They knew that during the summers of 1915 and 1916, the cotton crop had been damaged by the boll weevil, and that floods during 1915 had made the situation worse. They also knew that cotton growers in Florida, Alabama, Georgia, Louisiana, and Mississippi suffered great losses that had left numbers of tenant farmers and sharecroppers without crops and jobs.

Agents were sent to the South to encourage black people to take jobs in defense plants, shipyards, steel mills, and meat packing houses. Sometimes agents would provide free railroad tickets as an additional incentive.

Thousands of black people began leaving the South to take jobs in Northern factories. Many of the new factory workers wrote back to relatives and friends telling them about their new jobs and good wages. With this added encouragement, the flow of blacks into the cities increased tremendously. They, too, came in search of factory jobs.

People began to wonder why such large numbers of black people decided to move North at this time. Why hadn't they left the South long before? There were many reasons why the Southern black had remained in the South. But the primary reason was that black people knew that the white immigrant was always hired first, leaving few, if any, jobs for them. Therefore, blacks had little hope of providing for themselves in Northern cities.

However, Emmett J. Scott, who had been a speech writer and close aide to Booker T. Washington, made an investigation to find the reasons for the migration during World War I. Dr. Scott found that black-owned newspapers that had wide circulation in the South carried advertisements for jobs in Northern cities. The advertisements noted the wages for the different types of jobs. There were many responses to these advertisements. To help the migration, the leading black-owned newspaper, *The Chicago Defender,* organized a Great Northern Drive which was planned for May 15, 1917. Again, the response was great.

Another reason for the migration north was the unwillingness of the Southern courts to give black people equal treatment. Scott wrote in his study:

Negroes largely distrust the courts and have to depend on the influence of their aristocratic white friends. When a white man assaults a Negro he is not punished. When a white man kills a Negro he is usually freed without extended legal proceedings, but the rule as laid down by the Southern judge is usually that when a Negro kills a white man, whether or not in self-defense, the Negro must die. Negro witnesses count for nothing except when testifying against members of their own race.

The fee system, which paid a sheriff for feeding prisoners, was considered another reason why black people left the South. Under this system, if the number of prisoners increased, the fees would also increase. Naturally, the system encouraged sheriffs to keep their jails filled with prisoners. However, it was black people who were arrested in large numbers for minor offenses. This was true especially in Jefferson County, Alabama, where the sheriff found ways of feeding the prisoners for less than the fee he received per man. He could then keep what was not spent for himself. In 1917, for example, the Jefferson County prisoners' fees totaled about $37,688, but the sheriff had spent only about one third of that amount, leaving approximately $25,125 for himself.

Added to the job opportunities in the North, increasing numbers of lynchings, poor transportation accommodations, and poor educa-

A painting by Jacob Lawrence (one of a series,) shows the great
Northern migration of Southern Negroes during World War I.

tion all made black people eager to leave the South and travel on the Great Northern Drive to the North — the Promised Land.

As expected, white Southerners became alarmed at the great numbers of blacks leaving for the North. They barred the sale of *The Chicago Defender* in several towns. But those who got hold of the paper passed the copy around to friends until it became ragged. Black people eagerly read the job advertisements and information about the South being a terrible place for them to live. The publishers of *The Chicago Defender* could print negative comments about the South because their businesses were located in the North. Black-owned Southern papers, however, did not dare print such harsh statements about whites or openly encourage blacks to leave.

A Black Community Forms

UNTIL ABOUT 1910, THE CENTER OF BLACK LIFE in New York City was in an area on the west side of Manhattan Island extending from 27th to 53rd Streets. But a larger community of black people was also developing in the section called Harlem.

In 1903, a black real estate man named Philip A. Payton encouraged white owners of a few houses on West 134th Street to rent apartments to blacks. Whites were moving farther north to the growing area of Washington Heights, leaving Harlem apartments vacant. The white owners of the houses were eager to rent the vacant apartments. They even hoped to get higher rents from black tenants.

Black families that could afford the higher rents often wanted to leave the slum conditions in which they were living. More and more

A drawing from the March, 1920 issue of The Crisis, voice of the NAACP. It is the tragic plight and cry of Southern blacks. For many blacks the flight to the North seemed the only way to escape the violence of Southern whites.

families came to Harlem and soon the black community spread into a large area.

Some whites became alarmed. They formed companies that bought property surrounding the houses where black families lived and would not rent apartments or sell houses to black people. In fact, one white company produced a circular that asked whites to join together to "get rid of colored people." Those whites who wanted to rent apartments or sell homes to blacks were sometimes discouraged by the Ku Klux Klan.

But black people formed their own companies, such as the Afro-American Realty Company, to buy property and to rent to other blacks. Soon black-owned newspapers were calling upon black people to buy and lease property in Harlem. Even ministers encouraged their congregations to buy property. But financially able black families found that whites refused to rent or sell homes to them in the better sections of the city. Eventually, Harlem became a community where black people with a variety of incomes lived in harmony, side by side.

Many Southern blacks who came North in search of jobs settled in Harlem. The newcomers found a variety of foreign-born black people in Harlem. There were French-speaking blacks from Haiti. Later, others came from Guadaloupe and Martinique. Those from Puerto Rico spoke Spanish. The largest group of foreign-born came from the British West Indies. Thus, the black community in Harlem was made up of a variety of cultures. The life styles, foods, and dress covered a range from African to European to American.

During the 1920's, Harlem became overcrowded. There was little housing left, and much of it was inadequate. There were fewer job opportunities since the war had ended. The schools were crowded. Soon Harlem became known as the "ghetto." This word was originally the name for the old European Jewish community where the inhabitants were kept in isolation. And the greatest problem, discrimination

A Harlem street scene in the 1920's. At this time, Harlem was rapidly growing from a thriving black community into an overcrowded ghetto.

against black people, kept them in poverty and locked into the black community.

Back to Africa

HARLEM GOT A NEW RESIDENT one day in March, 1916. He was a twenty-nine-year-old Jamaican named Marcus Garvey, and he had a definite aim. He planned to start a chapter of his organization, the Universal Negro Improvement Associations, in America. In 1914, he had founded the association in Jamaica, British West Indies, and now he was ready for black Americans to join with him.

Garvey toured America, visiting thirty-eight states. He wanted to see first-hand how black people lived. He traveled through the Northern cities where black newcomers from the South had settled. And he went South to visit the places from which the Southerners had come. While in the South, Garvey visited Booker T. Washington, whom he had long admired.

Garvey also went to see W. E. B. Du Bois and the NAACP in New York. But he felt that Du Bois and the NAACP staff were too closely involved with whites, whom Garvey did not trust. He believed that they gained control over black causes and organizations and were not really interested in the masses.

After visiting different parts of the United States where there were large numbers of blacks, Garvey found that the masses were still poor. He felt that they were disorganized and needed a new leader. Garvey decided that he was going to be their leader.

But Garvey found that it was not easy to get the masses to listen

Marcus Garvey, founder of the Universal Negro Improvement Association (UNIA) and the "Back to Africa" movement, as he appeared in a parade around 1922.

to him. They considered him a foreigner and not their leader. However, Garvey did not give up. He used the street corners and meeting rooms in churches as gathering places where he could reach as many people as possible. He emphasized the necessity for black businesses, pride in being black, unity among blacks, and a desire to return to Africa.

He established the New York Universal Negro Improvement Association and became its president-general. To attract the poor the Association provided death and sick benefits for its members. To help support the program, each member paid thirty-five cents a month in dues. The central office of UNIA received ten cents, and the remainder stayed in the local chapter's treasury. By 1919, Garvey claimed that there were thirty chapters of the UNIA. He had won over thousands of poor black people.

Garvey wasted little time in following through with his program. He asked the League of Nations for permission to establish a colony in Africa. Then he contacted authorities in Liberia, an African country, to seek entry. He received a refusal from Liberia. In response he organized the Universal African Legion, whose purpose was to drive whites out of Africa.

Garvey established another enterprise, the Negro Factories Corporation. Only blacks could buy shares of the corporation for five dollars each. The money was to be used to build and operate factories in the United States, Central America, the West Indies, and Africa. No foreign businesses opened, but there were several businesses and a hotel in New York.

Then Garvey announced plans to form a steamship company. Its purpose was to link the black people of the world through commerce and to transport those who wanted to go to Africa. In June, 1919, the Black Star Line was established and shares were sold, also for five dollars. Three ships were bought, but each one needed extremely costly repairs and met disaster. The first was sold at auction by a judge's order at about ten percent of its original cost. The second sank in the Hudson River, while docked at a New Jersey pier. Though the third ship succeeded in making a trip to Cuba, it then broke down and was abandoned.

About three hundred thousand dollars were lost through the Black Star Line. Yet Garvey insisted that his followers' investments were safe. In 1923, Garvey was charged with using the mails to obtain money dishonestly for his steamship line. He was found guilty and sentenced to five years in prison. He was pardoned in 1927 and deported to Jamaica.

Garvey tried to revive his organization in Jamaica and later in London but was unsuccessful. The back-to-Africa movement died, and Garvey himself never got to Africa. He died in London in 1940. However, Garvey had made a great impression upon black people, and many of his followers remained loyal to him and to his ideas.

The Red Summer

BLACK AMERICANS did not need Marcus Garvey to remind them of their African roots. In 1919, three hundred years after a group of Africans arrived in Jamestown, black Americans celebrated the event. Throughout the United States, there were programs citing the efforts and achievements of black people. Some programs expressed the hope that blacks and whites would have better relations in the future. Other programs were less hopeful and focused on the problems of the times. Among these problems were the twenty-five riots that occurred during the last six months of 1919.

Many white workers feared that the growing number of blacks moving to Northern cities would increase the competition over jobs. In Chicago alone, the black population had increased from 44,000 in 1910 to over 100,000 in 1918. Race riots occurred in such cities as Boston, Omaha, Tulsa, and Washington. But the worst riot took place in Chicago. During five days of active rioting, 38 persons died and over 500 were injured. About 1,000 persons were made homeless and approximately $250,000 worth of property was destroyed.

The casualties and property loss was so high that Governor Frank Lowden of Illinois appointed the Chicago Commission on Race Relations to investigate the reasons for the riot and to make recommendations. The Commission charged that both blacks and whites, as well as government agencies, were responsible for the conditions that produced the riot.

The members recommended that several conditions be corrected. Specific suggestions were made about improving conditions in police protection, discrimination in arrests of blacks, housing, garbage disposal, education, public facilities, labor unions, and in reporting incidents of racial disturbances. Finally, the Commission recommended that the word "Negro" be spelled with a capital 'N' and the word "nigger" should not be used.

For the next twenty years such organizations as the Urban League and the YMCA used the Commission's recommendations as a basis for their programs.

Fraternities and Sororities

EARLY IN THE TWENTIETH CENTURY, young black students on white college campuses found that they were excluded from most activities. At Cornell University, eight black male students began meeting in 1905 to discuss their isolation as a group. They decided to organize a fraternity to help them develop brotherhood and keep close associations with each other. On October 27, 1906, Henry Arthur Callis

A Chicago street scene during the race riots of 1919. Sticks, planks of wood, broken bottles — any readily obtained objects — were used as weapons by both blacks and whites. The losses were heavy in both human life and property.

suggested they call their organization Alpha Phi Alpha. This was the first black Greek letter organization in America. During the next year, the Beta chapter of Alpha Phi Alpha was formed on the predominately black Howard University Campus.

College fraternities appealed to black students on other campuses. In 1911, Kappa Alpha Psi was established at Indiana University and Omega Psi Phi was formed at Howard University. Three years later, Phi Beta Sigma was organized at Howard.

Since few black female students were found in Northern colleges at this time, it is not surprising that no black sororities were formed at white Northern universities. However, black women students also felt that they needed organization similar to the men's fraternities. During the next two decades three were established at Howard University: Alpha Kappa Alpha in 1908; Delta Sigma Theta in 1913; and Zeta Phi Beta in 1922. In 1924, Sigma Gamma Rho was formed at Butler University.

In succeeding years, chapters of the black fraternities and sororities were found on the campuses of most white Northern universities. Through these organizations black students participated in a variety of programs to help their people. In 1920, the fraternity, Alpha Phi Alpha, established a "Go-to-High School, Go-to-College" program. The program was considered so effective that the fraternity launched another program called "Education for Citizenship," which encouraged blacks to vote. In 1929, the Delta Sigma Theta sorority established a vigilance committee to keep in touch with political and social issues that would help improve the conditions of black people. There were other programs to end segregation in Southern white universities, scholarships for black undergraduate and graduate students, public health projects, vocational education programs, and other general social action programs.

Although there were black fraternities and sororities, the organizations did not exclude whites. As early as 1914, Delta Sigma Theta initiated its first non-black member. The other fraternities and sororities followed by discarding their black only or racial clauses. However, black fraternities and sororities continued to be dominated by blacks, and similar white organizations remained segregated.

Blues and Jazz Evolve

NO ONE KNOWS EXACTLY WHEN IT BEGAN, but black people in the South were singing the blues before 1900. Blues music is distinguished from other types of music by its form and by its special sound, the "blue note." The blues is sometimes described as a way of singing about life. The music is often sad but at times it holds humor and a challenge to life. The words are about hard times — about losing a lover, having no money, landing in jail, being homesick, being tired, and, in general, having problems that create misery. Each blues singer molds the song according to his or her individual feelings. In fact, singing the blues becomes a way of relieving the singer's misery and making life bearable again. A good blues singer gives the "blue note" special treatment, draws the listener into the mood of the song, and shares the experience.

Some people say that the blues is a combination of the rhythmic shouts and field hollers of slaves, mournful songs of the dock workers, and the sorrowful spirituals. Others say that the blues can be heard in the gospel songs that developed in black churches.

Among the very early blues singers were Blind Lemon Jefferson, Blind Boy Fuller, and Peg Leg Howell. They sang country blues. However, William Christopher Handy was the first man to make the blues popular. Although Handy was a cornet player and not a singer, in 1903 he was inspired to use this form of music after hearing a black man in a Mississippi train station sing blues as he accompanied him-

self on a guitar. The guitar seemed more suited to blues singing than the banjo, which was popular then because the strings could be played with a twang that was much like the singer's voice.

Singers such as Ma Rainey and later Bessie Smith perfected the blues style and became professional blues singers. They sang what was called city, or "classic," blues. Soon band instruments were used along with the guitar as classic blues singers continued to shape the basic blues form.

In 1909, Handy wrote "Memphis Blues" as a campaign song for Edward H. Crump, a candidate in the city's mayoral elections. Crump won and the lively tune became a craze. Long after the election, people sang the "Memphis Blues" and whenever Handy's band played it, everyone went wild.

In 1912, Handy himself published a thousand copies of the "Memphis Blues." When it did not sell well he sold nearly all the copies and the rights for one hundred dollars to T. C. Bennett, a white music promoter in Memphis who had the music simplified and republished in New York, where it sold in large quantities. According to law, Handy would have to wait twenty-eight years before owning the copyright again. While Handy could not receive any royalties from that song, he continued writing and playing the blues. In 1914, his very successful "St. Louis Blues" was published, and soon he was known as the "Father of the Blues."

White-owned companies began recording blues songs. Soon they found financial success from the large numbers of blues records bought by black people. Blues recordings were known first as "race records" because they were produced especially for black people. But white people also began to buy the records and to listen to the blues.

Bessie Smith was a leading classic blues singer. Her records were

W. C. Handy, who became known as the "Father of the Blues."

35

sold almost as fast as they could be produced. Such great musicians as Louis Armstrong and the Fletcher Henderson band accompanied her on the recordings. During the late 1920's, another blues singer named Ethel Waters was performing in nightclubs.

Out of the blues came another form of music called jazz. It began among black marching bands in the South, some say in New Orleans. After World War I, many musicians were among the black people migrating to Northern cities in search of jobs. They brought the beginnings of jazz with them.

At this time, black musicians in the North were playing dance music in ballrooms. Both white and black people were dancing the turkey trot, the fox trot, the one-step, and the castle walk. But the Northern musicians also began playing jazz and in doing so, helped make the new music popular.

Jazz continued to develop during the 1920's. As the large Northern dance bands acquired more Southern musicians, they became jazz bands. By the end of the 1920's, every large Northern city with a black population of over sixty thousand, except Philadelphia, had a leading jazz band. In Chicago, there was Louis Russell and Louis Armstrong; in Baltimore, Chick Webb; in Memphis, Jimmie Lunceford; in Washington, Duke Ellington; and in New York, Fletcher Henderson among several others.

Blacks and the Theater

BLACK ACTORS AND ACTRESSES found few opportunities to work in serious dramas on Broadway. There were, however, several black performers working in comedies. Since most black dramatic actors were kept from performing on Broadway, several small black theatrical companies were established around the country.

The Fletcher Henderson band in the late 1920's. When Louis Armstrong joined the band in New York City, Henderson suggested that he switch from cornet to trumpet, the instrument for which Armstrong became famous.

In 1914, Lester Walton formed the Lafayette Stock Company in New York City. The company gave black performers an opportunity to work entire seasons in plays ranging from such classics as *Othello* and *The Count of Monte Cristo* to popular Broadway hits.

The Lafayette Stock Company provided excellent training that sometimes led to Broadway or Hollywood. Among the performers, those who finally were accepted by white producers were Charles Gilpin, Clarence Muse, Frank Wilson, and Evelyn Ellis. Other Lafayette performers appeared in such black companies as the Lincoln Theatre in Harlem, the Perkin Theatre in Chicago, the Standard Theatre in Philadelphia, and the Howard Theatre in Washington, D.C.

According to James Weldon Johnson, April 5, 1917, is the most important date for black people in the history of the American theater. On that date, three one-act plays opened at the Garden Theatre in downtown New York. They were *The Rider of Dreams, Granny Maumee,* and *Simon the Cyrenian.* J. Rosamond Johnson conducted members of his all-black Clef Club, which played and sang the music for the plays. The show was a success. James Weldon Johnson said that this was "the first time anywhere in the United States for Negro actors in the dramatic theatre to command the serious attention of the critics and the general press and public."

In 1920, *The Emperor Jones,* by white dramatist Eugene O'Neill, opened on Broadway with the black actor Charles Gilpin playing the lead part. Critics called Gilpin one of the ten best actors of that year. The play was O'Neill's first hit, and it gave black performers an opportunity to be accepted in serious drama.

Other plays also brought black performers to the attention of the white theater world. Among them were O'Neill's *All God's Chillun Got Wings* with Paul Robeson; Laurence Stalling's *Deep River* with

Above: Actor Charles Gilpin.
Below: Paul Robeson and Freddie Washington in the 1926 play, Black Boy.

Noble Sissle (right) and Eubie Blake, well-known writers
of the successful musical comedy, <u>Shuffle Along</u>.

Rose McClendon; Jim Tully's *Black Boy* with Freddie Washington; DuBose Heyward's *Porgy* with Frank Wilson, Evelyn Ellis, Georgette Harvey; and Marc Connelly's *Green Pastures* with Richard B. Harrison. *Green Pastures* received a Pulitzer Prize in 1926. It had the longest Broadway run of any play with black performers, and its choral director, Hall Johnson, was commended for his arrangements of the spirituals sung throughout the play.

While black actors were receiving acclaim in the 1920's, they usually appeared in works by white playwrights. But at the end of the decade limited opportunities arose for black playwrights. In 1929, Wallace Thurman's play *Harlem* opened, but only after a white man was credited as co-author. It was billed as *Harlem,* by Wallace Thurman and William Jordan Rapp. That same year, Garland Anderson received full credit when his play *Appearance* opened on Broadway. It seemed that black writers would finally see their work produced with proper credit on Broadway. A few years later, in 1933, Hall Johnson's *Run, Little Chillun* also opened on Broadway. The music was outstanding. Hall Johnson's real fame, in fact, came from his musical ability and great knowledge of spirituals. His father was a free man who became a minister and later, a college president, but his mother and grandmother were former slaves. They provided Johnson with his knowledge of spirituals.

Many other black people might have created dramatic works at that time if it had been easier to get them produced. Several years had to pass before much serious drama by black writers was to appear on the American stage.

In musical comedy, *Shuffle Along* opened in 1921 at the 63rd Street Theatre, located off-Broadway. It was really written for black audiences. Two black partners, Noble Sissle and Eubie Black, wrote the lyrics and music for the musical. The show had a successful two-year run and the star, Florence Mills, was an obvious hit. Others in the show, such as Josephine Baker in the chorus line and Hall Johnson and William Grant Still in the orchestra, later became well-known.

Black theatrical figures were being seen frequently and were receiving more recognition. But at the same time, other blacks were receiving notice for their performances on the concert stage.

New Talent in Concert

A MOVEMENT TO TRAIN TALENTED YOUNG MUSIC STUDENTS began in the United States after World War I. In the East, three outstanding new music schools opened: the Eastman School of Music in Rochester, New York (1921); the Juilliard School of Music in New York City (1923); and the Curtis Institute of Music in Philadelphia (1923). These schools all became leading music institutions that gave young men and women the opportunity to receive training that in the past could have been had only in Europe.

Black people, however, were already studying music seriously and giving concerts before these schools were established. Their churches were the traditional place to perform — in concerts, in choirs, and in music competitions. Black churches and schools sponsored promising talent in concerts and raised money to help pay for advanced study. Some black musicians joined faculties of black colleges, where they trained young people, conducted orchestras and choruses, and tried out new compositions.

Before the 1920's, a few black men and women began appearing on concert stages in the United States and in Europe. Among those of note was a young man from Curryville, Georgia, named Roland Hayes. He began giving concerts in 1917, at the age of thirty. While Hayes was praised by critics, attendance at his concerts was poor. Hayes left for Europe, where he gave a command performance be-

Singer Roland Hayes receives the Spingarn Award in 1924 from Joel E. Spingarn
as James Weldon Johnson, who received the award in 1925, looks on.

fore the King and Queen of England and won international recognition. When he returned to the United States in 1923, he was well received. His concert at Symphony Hall in Boston in December, 1923, was the beginning of a long, rewarding career.

Paul Robeson, another black singer, had already distinguished himself in the theater, both as an actor and as a singer. Although he had not studied voice, Robeson's first concert in 1925 at the Greenwich Village Theatre in New York was a tremendous success. Other concerts, dramas, and musicals followed, making Robeson a star both in the theater and on the concert stage.

One young singer who received financial help from her church for private advanced study was Marian Anderson. While still in her teens, the promising young Philadelphian, who was born in 1902, was heard by Roland Hayes. He took an interest in her career, encouraged her to continue studying, and a few times he even sang with her. In 1924, Marian Anderson was among more than three hundred talented musicians in a competition held by the New York Philharmonic Symphony Orchestra. She won first prize. In 1929, she received the Julius Rosenwald Fellowship, which helped pay for further study in Europe. Marian Anderson became one of the world's leading singers.

Black composers and choral conductors were also emerging. Robert Nathaniel Dett had made a name for himself as pianist, composer, arranger, and choral conductor. Dett was born in Quebec, Canada, in 1882. Since the black community there had been established by runaway slaves, young Nathaniel, as he was usually called, heard the spirituals and other songs that originated in the Southern part of the United States. After studying at leading music conservatories in the United States and in Europe, Dett, as conductor of the Hampton Institute Choir, performed at the Library of Congress, Carnegie Hall in New York, and Symphony Hall in Boston. In 1930, he took the choir

Robert Nathaniel Dett, well-known pianist, composer, arranger, and choral conductor.

on tour in Europe. The next year they toured the United States. Dett and the Hampton Institute Choir were well received in both Europe and the United States.

Through the years, Dett continued to compose choral works for piano, arrange spirituals, and train choral groups at other colleges where he worked. He received several awards in recognition of his contributions to American music. Among them were the Bowdoin Prize at Harvard in 1920 and the Harmon Foundation Award for composition in 1927. The Eastman School of Music awarded Dett an honorary Master of Music degree. Oberlin and Harvard Universities gave him honorary doctorates in music.

Another composer and arranger of the time was William Levi Dawson, born in 1898 in Anniston, Alabama. After studying at Tuskegee Institute, Chicago Musical College, and the American Conservatory of Music, he returned to Tuskegee as the director of music and conductor of the choir. Dawson also won awards for his choral works and arrangements of spirituals. The Tuskegee Institute choir with Dawson as conductor became well-known throughout the country.

By the late 1920's, black choruses were appearing on the concert stage as often as black soloists. Hall Johnson and Eva Jessye became well-known choral conductors. Johnson studied at several schools around the country. Among them were the Institute of Musical Art and the University of Southern California. He studied the piano but became a professional violinist. Johnson, however, realized that his real love was choral conducting. In 1925, he formed the popular Hall Johnson Choir.

Eva Jessye, born in 1895, organized her first singing group — a girls' quartet — at age twelve. Eva's parents encouraged her interest in music. Eva studied choral music and theory and sang in choirs

Hall Johnson, who formed and conducted the popular Hall Johnson Choir.

and other groups. After graduating from Langston University in Oklahoma, she taught music in the Oklahoma public schools and later at Morgan State College in Maryland.

In 1922, Eva Jessye went to New York where she finally organized the Original Dixie Jubilee Singers. Later the group was called the Eva Jessye Choir. The choir was soon in great demand and appeared on such radio programs as *Major Bowes Family Radio Hour* and the *General Motors Hour*.

Eva Jessye went to Hollywood in 1929 to train a choir for the film *Hallelujah*. About four years later, she was the choral director for *Four Saints in Three Acts,* a production of the well-known white composer Virgil Thompson.

Undoubtedly, both black soloists and choral groups had made a name for themselves on the concert stage. Some became known nationwide through films and radio. At last, serious black musicians were receiving well-deserved recognition.

The "New Negro"

THE PHRASE, "NEW NEGRO," had been used as early as 1895 in an article in the *Cleveland Gazette*. On June 28, the article noted that "a class of colored people, the 'New Negro' who have arisen since the war, with education, refinement and money" had obtained the passage of a New York Civil Rights Law. The phrase came into greater use when in 1925 Alain Locke, a black man, edited the book *The New Negro: An Interpretation.*

Locke had received a Ph.D. from Harvard, had been elected to Phi Beta Kappa, was a Rhodes Scholar, did further study at the University of Berlin, was a professor at Howard University, and later wrote numerous articles and books. Locke felt that many young black people had the ability to become outstanding in their chosen fields. He saw to it that some of their ideas and works were published in his book. There were articles, essays, poems, and stories written by the young "New Negro" blacks.

In addition, Locke illustrated the difference between the old Negro and the new Negro. He wrote of the "Old Negro:"

The day of "aunties," "uncles" and "mammies" is equally gone. Uncle Tom and Sambo have passed on, and even the "Colonel" and "George" play barnstorm roles from which they escape with relief when the public spotlight is off. The popular melodrama has about played itself out, and it is time to scrap the fictions, garret the bogeys and settle down to a realistic facing of facts.

The "New Negro," Locke continued,

. . . wishes to know for what he is, even in his faults and shortcomings. He resents being spoken of as a social ward or minor, even by his own, and to being regarded a chronic patient for the sociological clinic, the sick man of American Democracy.

Along with the emerging writers and artists of the Harlem Rennaissance came other black leaders who could also be called the "New Negro." They pointed out the need for unity, race pride, self-respect, self-help, and full citizenship.

Carter G. Woodson realized that to develop racial pride it was necessary for black people to know their history and culture. However, most black people had little opportunity to learn about their past. Little was written and schools did not teach about black people. To correct the situation, Woodson organized the Association for the Study of Negro Life and History in 1915. Because many black people felt that the word "Negro" was degrading, the association changed its name, in 1972, to the Association for the Study of Afro-American

Life and History. Scholars did research and presented their findings at association meetings. Some of their research was printed in journals and books. In addition, Woodson started "Negro History Week," which was celebrated in schools through programs that noted the achievement of outstanding black people. Woodson's efforts called attention to the history of black people, but there was still need for other kinds of activities to present black people in a more favorable light and to help develop black pride.

Another of these black men who deeply felt the need for black people to know and understand their history and culture was Arthur A. Schomburg. He was born in Puerto Rico in 1874 and came to the United States mainland in 1891. Schomburg began collecting books and other written materials about his people. In a speech at Cheyney Institute, Schomburg suggested that blacks learn Arabic because the African culture, history, and tradition influenced their lives. He also urged that blacks develop racial pride and called for schools to include Negro history in their curriculums.

Schomburg also felt that "For him [the black man] a group tradition must supply compensation for persecution, and pride of race the antidote for prejudice." As Schomburg's feelings and ideas grew firmer, he decided to share his collection. So in 1926, through the efforts of the New York Urban League, it was placed in the New York Public Library. By that time, the collection included autographs, rare books, prints, and manuscripts dealing with the history and culture of black people. Schomburg became curator of the division in which his books and other materials were placed. The widely used materials are still in the Schomburg Collection of Negro Literature and History of the New York Public Library.

Schomburg was only one of the large number of black people who came to Northern cities to improve their conditions through education and better paying jobs. Larger numbers of black people were earning wages closer to those of whites. Therefore, black communities were beginning to be like white communities. There were poor people, middle class people, and a few who could be called rich.

During this period of change, a successful black person was now known as an outstanding writer, an outstanding scientist, an outstanding musician, an outstanding educator, or an outstanding scholar and not just "an outstanding Negro."

Most of the new leaders or the "New Negros" were born and reared in the South. Some had once been slaves; others were children of former slaves. In the few years since slavery had ended, many black people made great strides toward developing abilities to create and to be leaders.

The black church continued to be the main producer of black leaders. Ministers such as Adam Clayton Powell, Sr., Francis J. Grimké, Robert E. Jones, and Reverdy Ranson, from among a group of about fifty, became involved in many civic activities outside their churches. Some became forces in such organizations as the NAACP and the Urban League. Still others worked in politics, businesses, and international church councils.

Black educators, who wanted their young people to have successful and satisfying lives, accepted contributions from wealthy whites to improve their schools. Funds were also set up for continuing aid to black schools. Despite the funds, the effect of the "separate but equal" decision of the famous *Plessy* vs. *Ferguson* case in 1896 kept the education of black students inferior to that of whites.

Some black educators, however, were outstanding in their efforts to provide a better education for black students. One such educator was Mary McCleod Bethune, who established the Educational and Training School for Negro Girls. Some years later the school merged with the Cookman Institute for Boys and became known as Bethune-Cookman College.

In labor, blacks also continued to face discrimination. A. Philip Randolph was one black leader who was not afraid to fight for equality in jobs. In the 1920's, he led a struggle to organize railroad porters and maids. In 1925, Randolph organized the Brotherhood of Sleep-

ing Car Porters, which became the strongest black labor group in the United States.

The last black Congressman, George H. White of North Carolina, had finished his term in 1901. He predicted in a speech that the Negro would return to Congress. However, it took twenty-seven years before another black man sat in the United States Congress. He was Oscar de Priest, a Republican of Chicago, who was sent to the House of Representatives in 1928. He came from a district that was about four-fifths black but which had a white Congressman who died after his renomination. A committee of five politicians including de Priest nominated him to fill the seat. De Priest had long been active in politics in the black community of Chicago. He spoke out for the rights of black people. While some blacks thought his manner was too coarse, de Priest was effective and he served two more terms.

Numerous other outstanding black men and women during this period also could be called the "New Negro." Each one worked in his or her own field to help black people improve their conditions.

Harlem Renaissance

NEW VOICES WERE HEARD IN HARLEM. Claude McKay, Jean Toomer, Countee Cullen, and Langston Hughes were considered the leaders

Left: Carter G. Woodson's work in the area of black history laid a solid groundwork for present-day historians. Center: Reverend Adam Clayton Powell, Sr., Pastor of St. Philips Episcopal Church in Harlem. Powell's church encouraged black people to move to Harlem by buying buildings and renting apartments. Right: Reverend Francis J. Grimké, a leading black minister in Washington, D.C. who was a nephew of the Grimké sisters, white abolitionists. Below: Mary McCleod Bethune established schools to provide better education for black children.

53

of the new black poets who lived and worked in the largest black community in America.

Claude McKay came from Jamaica, British West Indies, in 1912 with the intention of studying agriculture. But he had already published two books in Jamaica. The first was published in 1911 when McKay was twenty-three years old; the second was published the next year. It is not surprising that McKay changed his mind about a career in agriculture. After two years at Kansas State University, McKay took a trip to England, where he published a collection of poems in 1920. His first American publication was *Harlem Shadows,* published in 1922. The book contained many poems from his previous books as well as several new ones.

McKay was a restless man who traveled a great deal and who lived in Europe for long periods of time. Eventually he turned to writing prose, but he was best known in America for his social protest poetry. His poem "If We Must Die" was written to protest lynching and violence against blacks in Southern states. Many years after it was written, Winston Churchill, Prime Minister of Great Britain, recited McKay's poem at the end of a speech aimed at persuading the United States Congress to vote in favor of entering World War II.

If We Must Die

If we must die, let it not be like hogs
Hunted and penned in an inglorious spot,
While round us bark the mad and hungry dogs,
Making their mock at our accursed lot.
If we must die, O let us nobly die,
So that our precious blood may not be shed
In vain; then even the monsters we defy
Shall be constrained to honor us though dead!
O kinsmen! we must meet the common foe!
Though far outnumbered let us show us brave,

And for their thousand blows deal one deathblow!
What though before us lies the open grave?
Like men we'll face the murderous, cowardly pack,
Pressed to the wall, dying, but fighting back!

In 1923, Jean Toomer's book, *Cane*, was published. While some critics considered it an extraordinary book, it did not have a wide circulation. But *Cane* had a great influence on young black Harlem writers. Toomer used poetry and prose in a new and different way to explore life through the eyes and experiences of black people. Some people said that the book was a blend of realism and mysticism. A member of an influential group of American poets said that parts of *Cane* "challenge some of the best modern writings." Toomer, himself, seemed to be searching for an identity. In response to a request for biographical information, Toomer, who was a grandson of P. B. S. Pinchback, the black politician who served for a time as lieutenant governor of Louisiana, wrote:

When his [P.B.S. Pinchback's] heyday was over, he left the old hunting grounds and came to Washington. Here I was born. My own father likewise came from middle Georgia. Racially, I seem to have (who knows for sure) seven blood mixtures: French, Dutch, Welsh, Negro, German, Jewish, and Indian. Because of these, my position in America has been a curious one. I have lived equally amid the two race groups. Now white, now colored. From my point of view I am naturally and inevitably an American. . . . Without denying a single element in me, with no desire to subdue one to the other, I have sought to let them function as complements. I have tried to let them live in harmony. Within the last two or three years, however, my growing need for artistic expression has pulled me deeper and deeper into the Negro group. And as my powers of receptivity increased, I found myself loving it in a way that I could

never love the other. It has stimulated and fertilized whatever crea-
tive talent I may contain within me. A visit to Georgia last fall was
the starting point of almost everything of worth that I have done.
I heard folk-songs come from the lips of Negro peasants. I saw the
rich dusk beauty that I had heard many false accents about, and of
which till then, I was somewhat skeptical. And a deep part of my
nature, a part I had repressed, sprang suddenly to life and re-
sponded to them.

After Toomer wrote the one book, he left Harlem. He turned to
the study of psychology and went to Wisconsin to experiment in the
subject with some friends. Some time later, Toomer moved to Bucks
County, Pennsylvania. He died in 1967.

Another well-known writer during the Harlem Renaissance was
Countee Cullen. He was born in New York City in 1903 and attended
the city's public schools. Later, at New York University, young Cullen
was a brilliant student. In 1925, during his last year at New York
University, Cullen published a book of poems titled *Color*. It won the
Harmon Foundation Gold Award for literature and received notice
among those interested in literature. A John Guggenheim fellowship
for creative writing enabled Cullen to study in France for two years.
He continued writing and became a public school teacher when he
returned to New York City. A sample of his poetry follows:

Incident

Once riding in old Baltimore,
Heart-filled, head-filled with glee,
I saw a Baltimorean
Keep looking straight at me.

Now I was eight and very small,
And he was no whit bigger,

And so I smiled, but he poked out
His tongue, and called me, "Nigger."

The giant of the new black poets was Langston Hughes, born in Joplin, Missouri, in 1902. As a youngster, Hughes enjoyed reading poems by the black poet Paul Laurence Dunbar. The poems were full of love for black people. They had a style and rhythm that young Hughes enjoyed.

Hughes's classmates recognized his ability to create poetry. When they were ready to graduate from grammar school, the class elected Hughes class poet. Then Hughes wrote his first poem.

He continued to write poetry throughout his teens. The words and rhythms came freely. At eighteen, Hughes wrote his now famous poems "I, too, Sing America" and "The Negro Speaks of Rivers." The second poem was dedicated to W. E. B. Du Bois, whose book *The Souls of Black Folk* was a great inspiration to Hughes.

Hughes sent his poems to various magazines hoping to be published. But he received them back with rejection slips. Hughes did not give up. He sent some prose and a few poems to a new children's magazine, *The Brownie's Book,* which was started by Du Bois and the staff of *The Crisis* magazine. Both the poetry and the prose were accepted and published. Du Bois and his staff also encouraged Hughes to continue writing.

Feeling more confident now, Hughes sent his poem "The Negro Speaks of Rivers" to the magazine staff. Much to his surprise, the poem was printed in the June, 1921 issue of *The Crisis*. This was the first adult magazine to publish his work.

The Negro Speaks of Rivers

(To W. E. B. Du Bois)

I've known rivers:

I've known rivers ancient as the world and older than the
    flow of human blood in human veins.

My soul has grown deep like the rivers.

I bathed in the Euphrates when dawns were young.
I built my hut near the Congo and it lulled me to sleep.
I looked upon the Nile and raised the pyramids above it.
I heard the singing of the Mississippi when Abe Lincoln
    went down to New Orleans, and I've seen its muddy
    bosom turn all golden in the sunset.

I've known rivers:
Ancient, dusky rivers.

My soul has grown deep like the rivers.

Only two magazines were willing to devote space to support the young Harlem writers. They were the publications of the NAACP, *The Crisis,* and the National Urban League, *Opportunity: A Journal of Negro Life.* Du Bois had tended to favor the older established black writers, even though he published Hughes's work and that of two other young black poets in *The Crisis.* As early as September, 1917, Roscoe Jamesons's "Negro Soldiers" and the next month, Claude McKay's "The Harlem Dancer" were published by Du Bois. McKay's poem was published under his pen name Eli Edwards.

Charles S. Johnson, editor of *Opportunity,* came across a poem by Countee Cullen that inspired him. While the magazine was supposed to deal with labor concerns of black people, a section was set aside to review current black literature. Jean Toomer's book, *Cane,* was given

Well-known poets,
above left: Claude McKay,
above right: Countee Cullen, and
below: Langston Hughes.

a long, favorable review. Many other black writers, such as Rudolph Fisher, Zora Neale Hurston, and Wallace Thurman, were discovered and given recognition in the magazine.

Through the magazine, *Opportunity,* the Urban League also offered awards to writers. Winners were announced at annual dinners held in large, well-known New York hotels. The awards and the attention given the winners created much excitement among the young black writers.

There seemed to be a need, however, for black writers to state their intentions. In 1926, Hughes published an article in the magazine *The Nation,* titled "The Negro Artist and the Racial Mountain." It became a kind of public declaration of the "New Negro" writer. Hughes stated in the article:

We younger Negro artists who create now intend to express our individual dark-skinned selves without fear or shame. If white people are pleased we are glad. If they are not, it doesn't matter. We know we are beautiful. And ugly too. The tom-tom cries and the tom-tom laughs. If colored people are pleased, we are glad. If they are not, their displeasure doesn't matter either. We build our temples for tomorrow, strong as we know how, and we stand on top of the mountain free within ourselves.

The young Harlem writers revealed much about black people and life in America. Alain Locke, the first black Rhodes Scholar, published several books on the life and culture of his people. He was also the editor of *The New Negro* (published in 1925), a collection of articles, essays, poems, and stories by several of the Harlem Renaissance writers. Among them are short story writers Rudolph Fisher, Jean Toomer, and Eric Walroad. In fiction, there are Jessie Fauset and Walter White, and in drama, Willis Richardson. Jessie Fauset's novel *There is Confusion,* published in 1924, explored the color line problem in America. *The Weary Blues,* Langston Hughes's first collection of poems, was published in 1926. In 1928, *The Walls of Jericho* by Rudolph Fisher presented the various types of black people living in New York.

The Harlem Renaissance writers became increasingly critical of their parents' generation. They looked in new directions for ideas. Above all, they demanded equal rights.

During the Harlem Renaissance, the work of young black artists also began to be accepted. Perhaps people were at last viewing black people other than as slaves or servants. One example of this change could be seen in a painting, *The Gulf Stream,* by the nineteenth-century artist Winslow Homer. The painting, which showed a black man as a strong figure, moved away from the traditional view of black people as singing and dancing slaves or as cotton pickers on the plantations.

Among young black artists, their own people were almost always the subjects of their work. A young black artist named Aaron Douglass was becoming known as an important painter. Douglass felt that painting had purposes similar to those of poetry. That is, paintings should record history, reveal thought, and transform myths. Douglass, like other young black artists, turned away from traditional subjects primarily to paint scenes of black people and places or to interpret the mood and spirit of the twenties.

Archibald Motley, another young black painter, who was born in New Orleans in 1891, used the ideas of the twenties more than any of the others. He also turned to Africa for inspiration. Instead of using African designs, Motley interpreted myths in his paintings. He also painted black people and Parisians in night life scenes.

James Porter became a leading interpreter of the facial expressions

Over: In <u>The Gulf Stream</u>, a painting by Winslow Homer, the central figure — a black man — is portrayed with dignity and strength.

of black people. Two of his well-known paintings are *Sarah,* which was destroyed in a fire, but there is a reproduction of the original, and *Woman Holding a Jug.* Porter, born in Baltimore in 1905 and educated in the public schools of Washington, D.C., graduated with honors from Howard University in 1927 and joined the art faculty there. While teaching at Howard, Porter continued studying art in New York and Paris. In later years, he began writing about black art and artists.

From Greensboro, North Carolina, came Malvin Gray Johnson. He was born in 1896 and died at the age of thirty-eight in New York City. Near the end of his short life, Johnson had reached the turning point of his career. After many disappointments and complete despair, the critics and the public were beginning to recognize his ability. Arrangements had been started for an exhibition of Johnson's work when he died. Some of Johnson's paintings of black urban and rural life are among the best records of the types of social life of black people. Although Johnson worked mostly in New York, he also painted black people in the deep South, revealing the beauty, tragedy, and color of the area.

The artist with an outstanding gift for design is Hale Woodruff. He was born in Cairo, Illinois in 1900, attended the Nashville public schools, and later studied at John Herron Art Institute in Indianapolis, Indiana. Woodruff's paintings and wood-block prints of blacks in America contain designs which sometimes make the social messages difficult to see and understand. However, his ability to combine design and scenes about the lives of black people gained attention. Woodruff's work was included in several exhibits during the 1920's. He joined the staff of Atlanta University and worked to make the university an art center. In 1946 Woodruff became professor of art at New York University. He still makes his home in New York City.

Sargent Johnson, born in Boston in 1888, became a notable black

Artist James Porter and his painting <u>Woman Holding a Jug</u>.

sculptor. Orphaned young and raised by his grandparents, young Sargent began modeling with clay from his own backyard. His models were the tombstone figures in a nearby stone-cutter's yard. Later, Johnson studied at the California School of Fine Arts. He painted and etched but preferred to sculpt. His work is outstanding for its simplicity, its sense of sureness and confidence. Johnson's ability to combine materials made his work even more distinguished. He worked in porcelain, terra cotta, woods, and metals. One work, *Pearl,* a statue of a child in blue-green porcelain and bronze, is an example of Johnson's ability to work in and combine different materials.

Born in Bay St. Louis, Mississippi in 1901, Richmond Barthé began studying at the Art Institute of Chicago in 1924. Barthé was a painter, but he enjoyed experimenting with sculpture. By the end of the 1920's, Barthé's sculpture began to receive recognition. He used black people as the subjects and in doing so made them acceptable in America. Later. Barthé's work received outstanding recognition both in the United States and in Europe.

Most black artists still were struggling fiercely to maintain themselves while working. Many years later, James A. Porter, one of the "New Negro" artists, wrote about their difficulties. In a newspaper article he wrote:

From 1900 to 1925 Negroes generally had to make their own opportunities in the Fine Arts. They had to wangle opportunities for study and travel and literally wheedle their way into the studios of white master artists under whom they wished to study. Later, to exhibit their work, they were forced to use the churches, the vestibules and reading rooms of public libraries and Y.M.C.A. buildings. Occasionally, they received help through well-intended race leaders, broad-minded educators, or white patrons of means.

Richmond Barthé and his statue of the Rug Cutters. "To cut a rug — "
meaning to go out and dance — was a popular expression used in the 1920's.

Self-taught black artists also produced work, but they often had to be "discovered." Without art teachers or influential friends to display their work in the appropriate places, many of these artists never received the recognition they deserved.

Horace Pippin, who was born in West Chester, Pennsylvania in 1888, was a self-taught artist. He understood art principles and used them in his paintings. As a soldier in France during World War I, Pippin kept diaries and made sketches of both the French countryside and the horrors of war. While most of his sketches were lost in battle, Pippin preserved six sketches in one of his diaries.

After being wounded in the shoulder and hospitalized in Europe, Pippin was returned to the United States in 1919. He never forgot his wartime sketches. In fact, he thought about them repeatedly. However, it was about ten years before Pippin produced any art work. But his early paintings illustrated the war scenes that he had kept in his memories. As he continued painting, Pippin turned from war to his experiences in West Chester, Pennsylvania and in Goshen, New York, two places of which he had fond memories.

Pippin was not "discovered" until he was forty-nine years old. At a West Chester County Art Association show, two of his paintings were praised by many people, including the famous illustrator N. C. Wyeth. Pippin's work was then shown at art shows in New York City and Philadelphia. But unfortunately Pippin painted only nine more years. He died in 1946 at the age of fifty-eight.

Awards for achievement in literature and art brought recognition to many of the leading young black writers and artists. In 1924, the Amy Springarn awards for achievement in literature and art were established. Three years later the Harmon Foundation awards for art, literature, and other fields were also established.

The stock market crash in October, 1929, had a disastrous effect on the Harlem Renaissance writers and artists who found it difficult to support themselves. Soon they began either to leave Harlem in search of new careers or to remain and find jobs that gave them an income.

Langston Hughes went to Russia with a group of blacks who planned to make a documentary film. Charles S. Johnson, editor of *Opportunity* and also a social scientist, had left the year before to teach at Fisk University. Zora Neale Hurston returned to Florida to continue writing. And Countee Cullen became a teacher in the New York City public schools, but he later published other works. Two other well-known writers, who died suddenly within a few weeks of each other, were Rudolph Fisher, a short story writer and physician, and Wallace Thurman, a novelist and playwright.

Some of the artists continued to struggle on with their work. For many, the lack of money was not new. But by 1930, the Harlem Renaissance had come to an end. Organizations such as the Urban League, which had helped young creative people, had to redirect their programs and available money to securing jobs and helping people through the depression. However, through public-works projects in the early 1930's, government aid was extended to black artists. Some taught art and others did art work on buildings financed by the government. But the flood of creativity of the Harlem Renaissance had dwindled.

Black Businesses

SOME FREE BLACK PEOPLE had run their own businesses during the eighteenth and nineteenth centuries. There were still black-owned businesses in the early 1900's. Mostly they provided personal services, such as barber shops, beauty parlors, and cleaning and pressing establishments. Other businesses, which were considered major achievements, were banks, life insurance companies, and newspapers.

Some black people felt that the power of black businesses and the accumulation of money would help end racial prejudice. Support for this opinion was found in Booker T. Washington's book, *The Negro in Business,* published in 1907. It contained a series of stories about successful black businesses.

Actually, there was a large growth in the number of black businesses after 1900. The National Negro Business League, of which Washington was president, noted that the total number had risen from 20,000 in 1900 to 40,000 in 1914. The number of black banks alone had grown from 4 to 51 during these fourteen years. Drug stores rose from 250 to 695 and retail merchants from 10,000 to 25,000. Of all the black-owned businesses, insurance companies became the most important and most successful.

The first center of black insurance companies was developed by fraternal societies in Virginia during the latter part of the nineteenth century. An emphasis among black people of that time on racial pride, self-help, and cooperation, helped many of their business efforts. While white insurance companies charged blacks higher premiums, black-owned insurance companies were fairer to black people. Black-owned companies paid sick benefits, which assured families of an income in case of illness.

Since one aspect of racial pride was to escape from the wage-earning class to become self-employed, capital and credit were needed to establish and operate businesses. However, white banks were reluctant to give loans to black people. But the push to own homes and run businesses made many black people seek the needed capital. Aside from high interest for the few loans they received, black people were suspicious of white-owned banks. After the Civil War, the Freedman's Bank, which was run by whites for black depositors, had collapsed. Many blacks received only about forty cents on the dollar and that was only after waiting for several years. In fact, the bank failed in 1874, and some depositors were still receiving only part of their savings in 1909. There was, however, an attempt to pass a bill in 1907, under which the government would reimburse the depositors for their losses. While the bill passed in the Senate, it was killed in the House of Representatives. At the time, Booker T. Washington said, "When they found that they had lost or been swindled out of their savings, they lost faith in savings banks, and it was a long time after this before it was possible to mention a savings bank for Negroes without some reference being made to the disaster of the Freedmen's Bank." W. E. B. Du Bois expressed the opinion that "the nation which robbed [the Negroes] of the fruits of their labor for two and a half centuries finally set them adrift penniless."

With this loss of faith in banks and the growing need for capital, many prosperous black businessmen were approached by other blacks for personal loans or were asked by poorer but thrifty blacks to "hold" their savings. Thus, black businessmen became bankers for other blacks in a very informal way.

In 1888, the first black-owned bank was established. It was called the Capitol Savings Bank and was located in Washington, D.C. The bank remained open for sixteen years. It finally collapsed because of bad risk loans and misuse of funds by bank officials. There were many other black banks during the following years, but like white-owned banks of the time, they also failed for the same reasons that closed the Capitol Savings Bank.

Between 1900 and 1928, twenty-eight black-owned commercial and savings banks were established in response to the economic needs of black communities. Although these newly established banks faced numerous barriers, several were able to survive. Black depositors proved to be thrifty, but they had, in general, small sums of money to place in the banks. Also pressure was often placed upon bank officials to give loans to some individuals who expected racial cooperation but were high risks. This type of situation placed bank officials in the position of choosing between protecting the bank and supporting the idea of racial pride.

Black pride was previously highlighted with the founding of the first black newspaper, *Freedmen's Journal,* in 1827. By the 1900's, the black press had developed into a vital force within black communities. Its editors and writers became community leaders. And in many instances, they were the "voices" of the black communities.

The black press demonstrated its leadership role in the black community through the kinds of information it passed on to black people. For example, information of importance to black people was always printed in the newspapers. Such newspapers as *The Chicago Defender* informed blacks in the South of the availability of jobs in the North after World War I. In many newspapers, magazines, and other printed materials, articles exposed threats, injuries, lynchings, and other injustices committed by whites against blacks and urged resistance to these wrong doings.

Other articles encouraged black people to cooperate with each other in order to survive the white racism that surrounded them. Self-help programs and activities were encouraged by black editors and writers. But most of all the black press told of the successes and accomplishments of black doctors, lawyers, teachers, and other workers. Through these efforts, the black press helped many black people to develop confidence in themselves and to help advance their people whenever possible. Through the years, the press continued to help black people survive in the hostile, white world of America.

A Sensational Case Begins

THE DEPRESSION had made thousands of men, women, and children homeless. About 200,000 of them either found shelter or became hoboes, traveling from place to place on freight trains.

The unveiling of The Chicago Defender's printing press in 1921. Robert S. Abbott, publisher and editor of this newspaper, (his mother is shown here) was one of the first journalists to use headlines.

The Scottsboro defendants. The one white youth wandered off and was never identified.

On March 25, 1931, about ten hoboes jumped aboard a train leaving Chattanooga on its way to Memphis. About half an hour after the train had left the first stop at Stevenson, the station master saw a group of hoboes. One of them was holding his bleeding head. Another of the hoboes said that there was a fight aboard the train and a "bunch of Negroes" had thrown them off. The station master called ahead to alert the station master at the next stop, Scottsboro, but the train had already left.

At the following stop, Paint Rock, the deputy sheriff waited at the station with orders to "capture every Negro on the train and bring them to Scottsboro." The sheriff had given him the authority to deputize every man in Paint Rock who owned a gun.

A few minutes before two o'clock in the afternoon, the freight train pulled into Paint Rock. The posse quickly climbed aboard. In a few minutes they found the hoboes. There were nine black youths, one white, and surprisingly, two young white girls dressed in overalls and wearing men's caps.

The black youths, ranging in age from thirteen to twenty, were rounded up and tied together. The two girls sat talking to some women who had gathered at the station. No one seemed to be paying any attention to the one white youth. About twenty minutes after the train stopped, Ruby Bates, the younger girl, asked to see the deputy. She told him that the nine black youths had raped them. The girls, however, gave little information about what was supposed to have taken place. Finally, the youths and the girls were taken to Scottsboro, where the youths were placed in jail and the girls were sent for medical examinations.

As word spread about the hoboes, white farmers and their families, including small children, began gathering at the jail. By late afternoon, there was a crowd of several hundred. Sheriff Wann called the governor, and twenty-five armed National Guard troops were sent to the jail. By the time the troops arrived at midnight, there were only twenty or thirty white men sitting in their automobiles around the area. A reporter on the *Birmingham News* tried to explain why the whites didn't remain at the jail. He wrote in the paper on June 8, 1931, "There were no relatives of the girls to feel surging in them the demand for blood vengeance. The question was one of race unheated by personal relationships."

This was the situation which was the basis for one of the most sensational trials in American history. Although the black youths pleaded innocent and one girl eventually said that she lied, the youths received the death sentence. After several years of trials, four of them were freed, and the remaining five were given long jail sentences.

A Shift in Politics

IN OCTOBER, 1929, THE STOCK MARKET CRASHED. Wages and prices fell. Banks collapsed and depositors lost their savings. Business owners began to fire employees. The Great Depression was on. As unemployment increased, so did the number of people standing in bread lines waiting for free food. Black and white people shared common problems — no jobs, no money, no food. Farmers had no buyers for the food they produced, so they, too, lost money. In addition, little rain fell on the plains and soon the dry, but good soil had blown away, leaving acres of farm lands unusable.

For the majority of the black population, who were also farmers, the beginning of the Great Depression made little difference. Those who had not joined the migration to the Northern cities after the war continued to live in poverty. Some of their farms were completely destroyed by the boll weevil. Others were left without an income producing crop because cotton cultivation had shifted from the Southeastern to the Southwestern states. Soil erosion also left numbers of

76

farmers with poor lands. Soon, both black and white farmers were forced to become either tenant farmers on more prosperous farms or to move to the cities in search of jobs.

Both black and white Americans looked to the government to pull the country out of the depression. But there was little faith now in President Hoover. He paid almost no attention to black people. There were fewer blacks in appointed office, and he remained silent about the numerous lynchings during his administration. Black people began to realize that their only hope for better conditions was in candidates who were sympathetic to their needs.

Black leaders were aware of a change in attitude toward blacks among Republicans. Since 1928, Republicans began to recognize whites as leaders in Georgia, Mississippi, and Texas and seated them instead of the black delegates at the National Convention. This new Republican policy angered many black leaders. Black-owned newspapers took up their cry and supported the Democratic presidential candidate Alfred E. Smith instead of Herbert Hoover. However, the Republicans were successful in getting Southern whites to vote Republican, and Hoover became president.

Black people realized that the Republican party no longer represented them. Soon they began using their votes to protest the actions of politicians. Records that showed how Congressmen voted on issues benefiting blacks were studied. Actions and policies of the President were also studied. Then methods of changing anti-black policies or actions were established. For example, John J. Parker was nominated for a position as judge on the United States Supreme Court. Black people made it known that Parker did not qualify to sit on the highest court because he had expressed the opinion that it was evil and dangerous to both races if black people participated in politics. The NAACP fought the nomination by holding mass meetings to alert people about Parker and to encourage them to send petitions to their Congressmen. Finally, the Senate decided not to confirm Parker's nomination. Then black voters turned their attention to the Senators who supported Parker. These Senators also felt the power of the black vote as it helped them lose when they ran for office again.

Other political party members saw that black voters were becoming dissatisfied with the Republicans and tried to attract them. The Socialist party already had such well-known members as A. Philip Randolph and Chandler Owen, co-editors of the black publication, *The Messenger*. Party members developed a program aimed at helping working people. Although most blacks were working people, the program was not aimed at solving the many different problems of black people. Therefore few blacks were attracted to Socialism.

The Communist party also tried to gain black members through an organized program. In 1925, they established the American Negro Labor Congress to bring together all black trade unionists. During the same year, they organized the International Labor Defense which concentrated on cases involving blacks. One such case was the sensational Scottsboro trial, which lasted for several years. Communists associated freely with black people to encourage membership in their party. The Communists allowed blacks to run for important positions in the party on state and national levels. In fact, James W. Ford, a black man, was the Vice-Presidential candidate in 1932 and the two succeeding elections. But the Communist party attracted only a small number of black people. Black voters did not find that socialism or communism could solve their problems.

By 1932, the hardships of the Great Depression were greatly felt by millions of black and white Americans. It was election time again, and large numbers of voters were among the unemployed. A Democrat named Franklin Delano Roosevelt was running against President Hoover. Roosevelt expressed a great deal of interest and concern for the jobless and poor and pledged a "New Deal" for them. The voters

The Depression: no work, no money, no hope. With the election of President Franklin D. Roosevelt in 1932, many blacks and whites received employment through the "New Deal."

paid attention and elected Roosevelt. Soon black and white people were listening to Roosevelt's fireside chats. They learned about his New Deal policies and began to benefit from his recovery program. Both black and white Americans looked to the new President to lead them into more prosperous times. And most black people left the Republican party and joined the Democrats. With this shift in political parties, some blacks said that Lincoln was now really dead.

Index

81

About the Author

FLORENCE JACKSON was born and raised in New York City. After receiving her B.S. degree from New York University, she went on for her M.S. degree at the City University of New York. She is now working toward a doctorate in urban studies at Fordham University. For several years, Ms. Jackson was a classroom teacher, a teachers' consultant, and an assistant principal. Presently she is Assistant to the Director of the Bureau of Social Studies of the New York City Board of Education, where she develops curriculum for the schools. Much of Ms. Jackson's work presently is devoted to the preparation of curriculum materials dealing with ethnic studies. Ms. Jackson lives in New York City with her two children, Karen and John, Jr., her mother, and their dog, Mitzi.